Feeling *Impatient* &
Learning *Patience*™

REAL

Annie's Jar of Patience™

SOPHIA DAY®

Written by Megan Johnson Illustrated by Stephanie Strouse

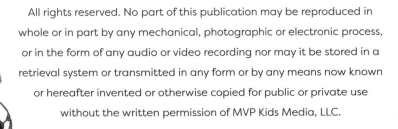

The Sophia Day® Creative Team-
Megan Johnson, Stephanie Strouse,
Kayla Pearson, Timothy Zowada, Mel Sauder

A **special thank you** to our team of reviewers who graciously
give us feedback, edits and help ensure that our products
remain accurate, applicable and genuinely diverse.

Published and Distributed by MVP Kids Media, LLC -
Mesa, Arizona, USA
Printed by Prosperous Printing Inc. -
Shenzhen, China

Designed by Stephanie Strouse

DOM Sept 2019, Job # 02-010-01

May your childhood be filled with adventure, your days with hope and your learnings with wisdom, and may you continuously grow as an MVP Kid, preparing to lead a responsible, meaningful life.

—SOPHIA DAY

"How many more days?" Annie asked her dad.

"You asked me yesterday, and I said three days. So, you tell me."

"Two more days!" Annie whined.

Annie was looking forward to spending time with her grandparents on Saturday. Her grandma said they might make kimchi from their garden.

Unfortunately, impatience took over her excitement. Her mind raced ahead to what she wanted to do. Her heart beat faster, as if it could make time go more quickly.

Even her body could hardly contain the anticipation.

At school, she fidgeted in her seat.

At home, she daydreamed,
missing out on things she could
have been enjoying.

Finally, Saturday morning came, and Grandpa Park picked her up.

The car ride into town was agonizing.

"Are we there yet, Grandpa?
We've been in the car *FOREVER!*"

"It's been twenty minutes. Just ten more."

Annie always seemed too bored with the present or too excited about the future to enjoy what was happening now.

Ten more minutes seemed like an hour.

When they finally arrived, Annie ran in the front door, through the living room, and straight out the kitchen door into the garden.

"I'm here! Let's make kimchi!"

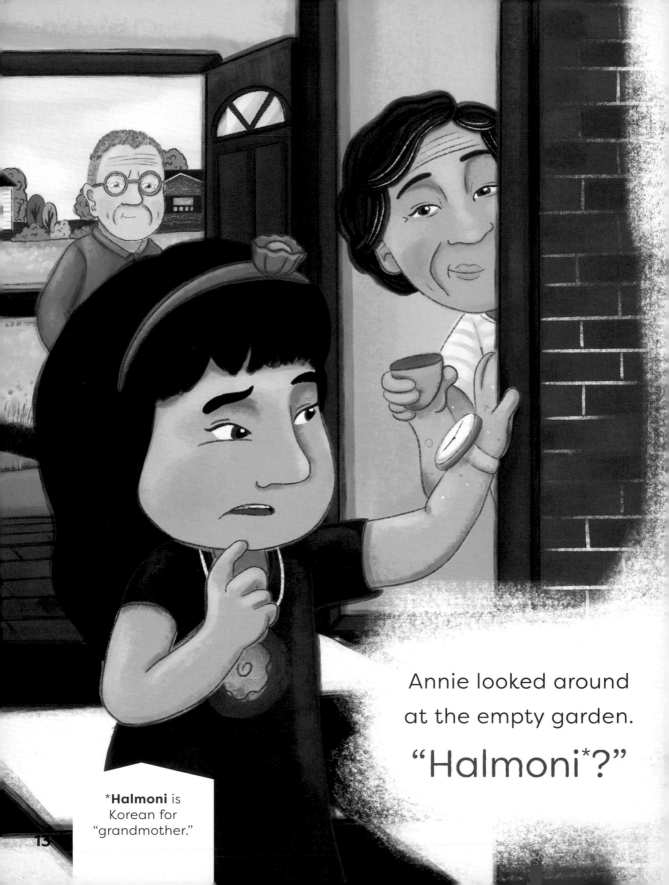

Annie looked around at the empty garden. "Halmoni*?"

*Halmoni is Korean for "grandmother."

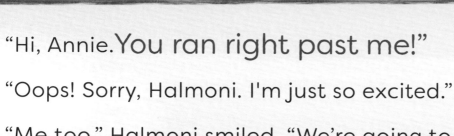

"Hi, Annie. You ran right past me!"

"Oops! Sorry, Halmoni. I'm just so excited."

"Me too." Halmoni smiled. "We're going to have a great day, but let's agree not to hurry past the good stuff. Deal?"

"Deal! So, can we make your kimchi today?" Annie asked.

Halmoni looked around the garden. "It's still too early for the cabbages and peppers," she said.

"When will they be ready?"

"About two more weeks, I'd guess."

"But I wanted to make kimchi **today!**" Annie complained.

Grandpa Park came out to help find a solution.

"Annie, you're a real go-getter. I appreciate your enthusiasm about making kimchi. I'm sorry the vegetables aren't ready. Let's find something else fun to do."

"But I don't want to do anything else!"
Annie whined.

"I hear that you're feeling impatient. Did you know that you can be in charge of your feelings? Just because you feel impatient doesn't mean you have to act impatiently."

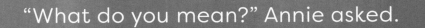

"What do you mean?" Annie asked.

"Whining doesn't solve anything, but when you feel that hurried, unhappy feeling, you can **think about your choices.**"

"You already said you don't want to choose to do something else, so another option is to look for a way to get what you want more quickly, a compromise."

"Like a shortcut? Aren't shortcuts bad?"

"Rushing through something and doing it carelessly will have poor results, but finding a good solution that's faster isn't wrong."

"So how do we make the garden grow more quickly," asked Annie.

Grandpa Park laughed.
"We can't rush the natural seasons.
Take a deep breath and try to think creatively.
If you must make kimchi today, is there another
way to get what you need?"

24

Annie had an idea, but she would have to decide if she was okay with trading Halmoni's home-grown vegetables for vegetables from the store.

"I wanted to use your garden veggies, but I *really* want you to teach me to make kimchi *today*," Annie told Halmoni. "Can we go to the store?"

"Okay," Halmoni agreed. "We'll harvest what we can and go buy the rest. It will cost more, but we can do it today. That's a good compromise."

Halmoni called out their list while Annie darted from bin to bin, picking up the ingredients—onion, garlic, ginger, cabbage. Annie's mouth was watering just thinking about the flavors.

Chilies were the last thing on their list. Annie **dashed off** toward the pepper section. She ran straight into another shopper, sending a carton of eggs **crashing to the floor!**

Garlic

Hot
Peppers

"Oh no! I'm sorry!" she exclaimed.

Annie grabbed another carton from the cooler and handed it to the man.

She grabbed the chili peppers and said,
"Let's go!"

"Not so fast," Halmoni said. "We're going to stay until the eggs are cleaned up."

Annie's heart beat faster and her mind raced. She noticed her feelings and remembered that just because she was feeling impatient didn't mean she had to act impatiently. She thought about her choices.

Grandpa was right that carelessness has poor results. Rushing to get the peppers actually made everything take longer. Annie wished they didn't have to wait for the worker with the mop. She picked up the egg shells to help the cleanup go more quickly.

Back at the house, they **took their time** to carefully chop the cabbage, shred the carrots, and slice the radishes. Annie didn't want to rush and get hurt.

They pressed the garlic, grated the ginger, and crushed the chili peppers.

They mixed it all together with the sauces and seasonings and scooped it into her grandmother's *onggi*, a special jar for preparing kimchi. Annie filled a second jar to take home to her family, too.

Annie saved one last spoonful for herself.

"Bleh!" Annie spit it out.

"What did I do wrong? This tastes awful!"

Halmoni laughed. "Oh, Annie! Kimchi, like patience, takes time to develop. The flavors form over time."

"I thought we would get to eat it *tonight.*" Annie said, disappointed.

"Not tonight. It will take about a week."

Annie almost whined, but she stopped. Acting impatiently wouldn't make a week go by more quickly.

"We can taste it together when I come over next week," Halmoni said.

"There's nothing we can do to make it faster?" Annie looked hopefully at Grandpa Park.

"No shortcuts this time, but you'll see it's worth the wait. Take this. While you wait, write down everything that makes you happy.

"The best way to develop patience is to
find joy in the process."

Annie took home her jar of kimchi and Grandpa Park's notebook. After a couple of days, Annie could smell the kimchi, making her mouth water. She laughed at the bubbles that danced when she tapped the jar.

PATIENCE IS KEY!
- Smells so good!
-bubbles tickle

Any time she was tempted to open it too early,
she remembered that just because she was
feeling impatient didn't mean she had to
act impatiently. She recorded things she was
thankful for and things she looked forward to enjoying.

When Halmoni and Grandpa Park came the next
weekend, they tested to see if Annie had been patient.
"How is the kimchi?" Halmoni asked.

"I don't know.
Let's find out!"
said Annie.

As Annie opened the jar, she realized that she was now part of a thousand-year-old family tradition, passed down from Halmoni and many generations before her. **Suddenly a week didn't seem so long!**

The first crisp, tangy bite of her very own kimchi was **worth the wait!**

You're a real go-getter, always in a hurry
To make the seasons change.
You just can't stand it when the circumstances
Don't go how you'd arrange.

Is what you're wanting worth the wait?
Or should you choose a different goal?
Is there a quicker compromise,
A shortcut or loophole?

When your goal just isn't fast enough,
You can choose to sacrifice
Some quality for speed,
If the tradeoff will suffice.

Time won't always go by quickly
Just because you're in a hurry.
You're likely to make more mistakes
While acting in a flurry.

So, keep your eyes set on your goal,
Or find a good distraction.
Patience comes through process,
Finding joy and satisfaction!

LEARN & DISCUSS

Annie is learning to understand impatience, evaluate her options and come to peace with waiting. Learn with Annie and discuss how you can develop patience, too!

When I was looking forward to going to my grandparents' house, my dad helped me see how many more days I had to wait. Sometimes we look forward to good things that are coming or being finished with things we don't like. Either way, waiting can be difficult!

What are you looking forward to right now?

What makes waiting difficult for you? What makes waiting easier?

Even though there wasn't anything I could do to make the time go more quickly, my impatience distracted me a lot. I missed out on some things I would have enjoyed because I was too busy thinking ahead.

What did I miss out on while I was daydreaming and feeling impatient?

Have you ever missed something you would have enjoyed because you were daydreaming?

When I finally got to Halmoni's house, I ran right past her to get to the garden! Sometimes, I'm so impatient about what I want that I forget to be kind or polite to others.

How do you think Halmoni felt when I ran past her?

Have you felt ignored by someone when they were focused on a goal?

How can you remember to show kindness, even when you're in a hurry?

I learned that impatience has a purpose. It helps us evaluate our goals. If something is happening too slowly, we have to decide if it is worth the wait. We can sometimes find a new goal instead. Making kimchi was really important to me, and I couldn't wait. I made a compromise and took a shortcut.

What compromise did I make?

When can taking a shortcut be a good choice? When can it be a bad choice?

How do you know when choosing a different goal or taking a shortcut is the best choice?

At the grocery store, I was in such a hurry that I caused a mess. I realized that hurrying doesn't always make things faster. Often, being in a rush causes problems, and our goals take longer because we hurried.

Have you ever made a mess or caused a problem by being in a hurry?

What might have happened if I had still been in a hurry while I was making the kimchi in the kitchen?

Grandpa Park gave me a notebook to write down the things that gave me joy while I waited for the kimchi to be ready. Instead of wishing away the days, I paid attention to notice what happened inside the jar. It was actually a lot of fun!

Pause everything you're doing to notice what's going on around you.

What do you see that is beautiful?

What do you hear that sounds nice? What is around you that is good? Slowing down to notice good things will help you develop patience.

How can you help your child understand impatience and learn to wait well?

Slow down. Our culture seems to glorify a hurried lifestyle that naturally cultivates impatience. We are accustomed to the instant gratification of electronics, the pressure to achieve and the glamour of recognition. Help your family slow down, unplug and be satisfied with the simple things in life such as nature, quality literature and time spent together. Place value on developing good character in addition to celebrating achievements.

Model patience. The best way to develop emotional regulation in children is modeling. First, consider how well you are doing with expressing patience, waiting well and keeping a balanced pace. Be honest with yourself, and if patience is one of your own struggles, it's likely you'll be sensitive to this trait in your child's behavior as well. Sometimes our own weaknesses become our greatest triggers in parenting. If you need to make a personal change in this area, talk to a friend about it. Expressing your goals out loud will help secure your commitment to personal change.

Encourage goal-setting. Patience is a discipline that is developed through practice. Children can be very good at living in the moment, causing meltdowns when reality doesn't match their expectations. By helping your child set goals, you reinforce the idea that the future is a product of many little choices. Good things don't just happen; they require a vision and hard work. Celebrate small milestones along the way to encourage patience with the process.

Facilitate structured practice. Set your child up for success in practicing patience by giving opportunities to wait. Instead of fulfilling a desire immediately, ask your child to wait for a short time. Increase the wait time as your child learns to wait well.

Help evaluate. When your child is expressing impatience, help evaluate the options like Grandpa Park did for Annie. When feeling impatient, a person has three options:

1. **Switch goals.** If what you want isn't happening quickly enough, perhaps you don't want it badly enough to wait for it. Is there something else you'd like to do instead?

2. **Switch methods.** If the way a person is working toward a goal isn't working quickly enough, maybe another method will work more quickly. Some people might call this a shortcut. Taking a shortcut is often seen as lazy, but it can be a viable option if time is limited. Switching methods or choosing a shortcut provide valuable opportunities for kids to evaluate the gains and losses of different ways to reach a goal.

3. **Come to peace with waiting.** If both the goal and the method of achieving it are important enough, there often isn't any choice but to come to peace with the situation and the timing. Distracting oneself with charting progress, noting simple joys or pursuing other pastimes can be helpful. These are the times in which one's patience is truly developed.

Meet the

mvpkids®

featured in
Annie's Jar of Patience™

ANNIE JAMES

BLAKE JAMES

Also featuring...

WILL PARK
"Grandpa"

SOOK-JA PARK
"Halmoni"

CHRIS JAMES
"Dad"

HANNAH PARK JAMES
"Mom"

JACKSON JAMES
Brother

LAYLA JAMES
Sister

Grow up with our MVPkids®

Our **CELEBRATE™** board books for toddlers and preschoolers focus on social, emotional, educational and physical needs. Helpful Teaching Tips are included in each book to equip parents to guide their children deeper into the subject of each book.

CELEBRATE!™
Board Books
Ages 0-6

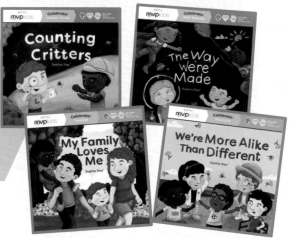

Our **Celebrate!™** paperback books for Pre-K to Grade 2 focus on social and emotional needs. Helpful Teaching Tips are included in each book to equip parents, teachers and counselors. Also available are expertly written curriculum and interactive e-book apps.

Celebrate!™
Paperbacks
Ages 4-8

Our **Help Me Become™** series for early elementary readers tells three short stories in each book of our MVP Kids® inspiring character growth. Each story concludes with a discussion guide to help the child process the story and apply the concepts.

help me BECOME
Early Elementary
Ages 4-10